CLASSROOM ASSESSMENT SCORING SYSTEM®

MANUAL INFANT

by

Bridget K. Hamre, Ph.D.
University of Virginia, Charlottesville

Karen M. La Paro, Ph.D.
University of North Carolina at Greensboro

Robert C. Pianta, Ph.D.
University of Virginia, Charlottesville

and

Jennifer LoCasale-Crouch, Ph.D
University of Virginia, Charlottesville

Baltimore • London • Sydney

Paul H. Brookes Publishing Co.
Post Office Box 10624
Baltimore, Maryland 21285-0624

www.brookespublishing.com

Typeset by Integrated Publishing Solutions, Grand Rapids, Michigan.
Manufactured in the United States of America by
Versa Press, Inc., East Peoria, Illinois.

Classroom Assessment Scoring System® (CLASS®) Forms, Infant, are manufactured in
the United States of America by H&N Printing & Graphics, Inc., Timonium, Maryland.
Classroom Assessment Scoring System® (CLASS®) Dimensions Overview, Infant, is
manufactured in the United States of America by H&N Printing & Graphics, Inc., Timonium, Maryland.

The *Classroom Assessment Scoring System® (CLASS®) Dimensions Overview, Infant,*
accompanies the *Classroom Assessment Scoring System® (CLASS®) Manual, Infant.* The
Classroom Assessment Scoring System® (CLASS®) Forms, Infant, are intended for one-time use
only and can be purchased in packages of 10 (ISBN-13: 978-1-59857-605-4). The *Classroom
Assessment Scoring System® (CLASS®) Manual, K–3* (ISBN-13: 978-1-55766-942-1),
Classroom Assessment Scoring System® (CLASS®) Manual, Pre-K (ISBN-13: 978-1-55766-941-4),
and *Classroom Assessment Scoring System® (CLASS®) Manual, Toddler* (ISBN-13: 978-1-59857-259-9),
are also available for purchase. To order, contact Brookes Publishing Co., 1-800-638-3775;
http://www.brookespublishing.com.

Library of Congress Cataloging-in-Publication Data
Hamre, Bridget K.
   Classroom assessment scoring system® (CLASS®) manual, infant / by Bridget K. Hamre, Ph.D.,
   Karen M. La Paro, Ph.D., Robert C. Pianta, Ph.D., and Jennifer LoCasale-Crouch, Ph.D.
      pages   cm
   Includes bibliographical references and index.
   ISBN 978-1-59857-604-7 (spiral)
   1. Early childhood education—United States—Evaluation.   2. Teacher-student
relationships—United States—Evaluation.   3. Classroom environment—United States—Evaluation.
I. La Paro, Karen M.   II. Pianta, Robert C.   III. LoCasale-Crouch, Jennifer.   IV. Title.
LB1139.25.H27 2014
372.21—dc23   2013038355

British Library Cataloguing in Publication data are available from the British Library.

2018   2017   2016   2015

10   9   8   7   6   5   4   3   2

Contents

About the Authors

Bridget K. Hamre, Ph.D., is Associate Director of University of Virginia's Center for Advanced Study of Teaching and Learning (CASTL). Dr. Hamre's areas of expertise include student–teacher relationships and classroom processes that promote positive academic and social development for young children, and she has authored numerous peer-reviewed manuscripts on these topics. This work documents the ways in which early teacher–child relationships are predictive of later academic and social development and the ways in which exposure to high-quality classroom social and instructional interactions may help close the achievement gap for students at risk of school failure. She leads efforts to use the Classroom Assessment Scoring System® (CLASS®) tool as an assessment, accountability, and professional development tool in early childhood and other educational settings. She has recently worked with leaders in several states and the Office of Head Start to implement the CLASS tool to enhance teacher–child interactions through accountability and professional development systems. Most recently, Dr. Hamre has engaged in the development and testing of interventions designed to improve the quality of teachers' interactions with students, including MyTeachingPartner and a 14-week course developed for early childhood teachers. Dr. Hamre received her bachelor's degree from the University of California, Berkeley, and her master's degree and doctorate in clinical and school psychology from the University of Virginia.

Karen M. La Paro, Ph.D., is Associate Professor at the University of North Carolina at Greensboro. She worked with inclusion projects and Head Start in Louisiana and received her doctoral degree in early childhood special education from the University of New Orleans. She worked for several years as research faculty with the *Eunice Kennedy Shriver* National Institute of Child Health and Human Development Study of Early Child Care and Youth Development as well as the National Center for Early Development and Learning at the University of Virginia. Her current research interests relate to issues of quality in early childhood classrooms and effective teachers. She works on projects and has published papers related to professional development for both in-service and preservice teachers.

Robert C. Pianta, Ph.D., is Dean of the Curry School of Education, Founding Director of the Center for Advanced Study in Teaching and Learning (CASTL), and Novartis U.S. Foundation Professor of Education at the University of Virginia, Charlottesville. A former special education teacher, Dr. Pianta is a developmental, school, and clinical child psychologist whose work focuses on how children's experiences at home and in school affect their development. He is particularly interested in how relationships with teachers and parents, as well as classroom experiences, can help improve outcomes for at-risk children and youth. Dr. Pianta is a principal investigator on several major grants, including MyTeachingPartner, the Institute of Education Sciences Interdisciplinary Doctoral Training Program in Risk and Prevention, and the *Eunice Kennedy Shriver* National Institute of Child Health and Human Development Study of Early Child Care and Youth Development. He is a senior investigator with the National Center for Early Development and Learning and Director of the National Center for Research on Early Childhood Education. He is the author of more than 200 journal articles, chapters, and books in the areas of early childhood development, transition to school, school readiness, and parent–child and teacher–child relationships, and he consults regularly with federal agencies, foundations, and universities.

Jennifer LoCasale-Crouch, Ph.D., is Research Assistant Professor at the University of Virginia's Center for Advanced Study of Teaching and Learning (CASTL). Her areas of expertise, in which she has authored multiple peer-reviewed manuscripts, include classroom observation, supporting children's successful transition to kindergarten, professional development that supports teachers' effective classroom interactions, and ways to implement such supports with high degrees of fidelity. Dr. LoCasale-Crouch has worked with the Office of Head Start in training staff to implement the roll out of the Classroom Assessment Scoring System® (CLASS®) and also has worked with multiple Head Start grantees across the country in their kindergarten transition planning development. Dr. LoCasale-Crouch is also a co-investigator on three recently funded Institute of Education Sciences grants designed to enhance the supportive ways teachers interact with children, particularly those at risk. Dr. LoCasale-Crouch received her bachelor's and master's degrees from the Florida State University, and she received her doctorate in risk and prevention in education sciences from the University of Virginia.

Contributors

Kristen Jamison, Ph.D.
Research Associate
University of Virginia

Sonia Cabell, Ph.D.
Research Scientist
University of Virginia

Bettina Viteri
Research Assistant
University of Virginia

Chalatwan Chattrabhuti
Research Assistant
University of Virginia

Beverly Sweeney, Ph.D.
Research Associate
University of Virginia

Acknowledgments

We gratefully acknowledge the support of Teachstone in the development of Classroom Assessment Scoring System® (CLASS®) Infant. We also thank the many teachers who welcomed us and allowed us to videotape and observe in their classrooms. Their dedication to improved practice is an example of their professionalism and care for infants.

Introduction

CHAPTER ONE

The Classroom Assessment Scoring System® (CLASS®) is an observation instrument that was developed to assess effective teacher–child interactions in infant, toddler, preschool, elementary, and secondary education classrooms and settings. The CLASS was designed to create a common metric and vocabulary that could be used to describe various aspects of effective teaching across grades and contexts. This manual provides information on the theoretical and empirical foundations of the CLASS, a summary of the CLASS dimensions as they relate to infants, an overview of the procedures for using the CLASS Infant tool, detailed descriptions and examples for each dimension as observed in classroom settings for infants, and a technical appendix of psychometric properties.

THEORETICAL AND EMPIRICAL FOUNDATIONS OF THE CLASS

The CLASS dimensions are based on developmental theory and research suggesting that interactions between young children and caregivers are a primary mechanism of child development and learning (Hamre & Pianta, 2007; Morrison & Connor, 2002; Rutter & Maughan, 2002; Sroufe, 1996; Thompson, 2006; Vygotsky, 1998). The CLASS dimensions included in the manual are based on interactions between teachers and infants in group settings; this system does not evaluate the presence of materials, the physical environment, issues related to health and safety, or the adoption of a specific curriculum or approach. This distinction between observed interactions and physical materials or reported use of curriculum or approach is important: the CLASS Infant tool specifically focuses on interactions between teachers and infants (i.e., how teachers engage and relate to infants as well as provide learning opportunities within activities and routines).

EFFECTIVE TEACHER–CHILD INTERACTIONS

Quality across education settings tends to be defined by structural and process variables. *Structural variables* generally include the features of settings and programs that can be easily regulated, such as materials available, teacher education, teacher–child ratios, and group size. *Process variables* tend to focus on dynamic aspects of the group setting,

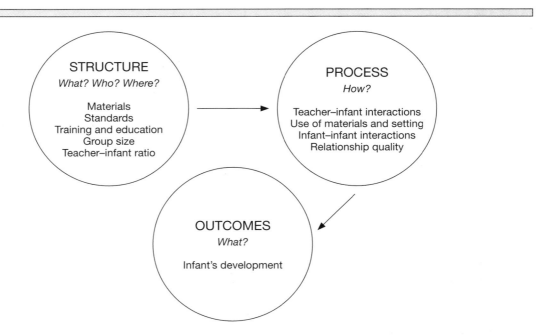

Figure 1.1.   Structure, process, and outcomes.

including teacher–child interactions, use of the materials in the setting to engage children, child-to-child interactions, and relationships. Although both the structural features and the process features of classrooms are important for children's social and developmental outcomes, research has shown that the structural quality is mediated by or flows through process quality (Mashburn et al., 2008). In other words, although it is important to have adequate materials for children and to have teachers who are highly educated, these features of the setting will only be as valuable as the teacher's use of them in engaging children and providing development and learning opportunities. The CLASS focuses on process quality, and the infant version examines teacher–infant interactions in the context of the unique needs of infants during this developmental period. A diagram representing this relationship of structural and process variables is shown in Figure 1.1.

INFANT DEVELOPMENT

Infancy is a period of intense development as infants learn how to interact with the world based on their primary relationships. Infants learn most of the skills they will need to navigate the world through interactions with others in their environment. These interactions contribute to their early relationships. Although initial relationships are typically established with a parent or primary care provider, as infants enter child care settings, important relationships are established with caregiving adults. Through positive interactions, these relationships foster social and emotional development and shape self-perception and self-regulation (ZERO TO THREE, 2008). Positive interactions between infants and adults can lead to healthy cognitive and social development (Nelson & Bosquet, 2005).

Recent evidence indicates the specific effects of positive interactions and subsequent relationships between infants and caregivers on later school readiness skills (Lally, 2010), communication skills (Raikes & Edwards, 2009), and socioemotional outcomes (Schore, 2005). For example, high-quality, consistent caregiver–infant interactions have been linked to executive function skills such as inhibition, working memory, and cognitive flexibility (Bernier, Carlson, & Whipple, 2010; Schertz & Odom, 2007; Thompson, 2009) as well as stimulated curiosity, exploration, and communicative intent (Ispa et al., 2004; Kochanska, Furman, Aksan, & Dunbar, 2005). Furthermore, consistent, high-quality interactions with adults positively affect infants' neurological growth and later cognitive and socioemotional outcomes (Burchinal, Vernon-Feagans, Cox, & Key Family Life Project Investigators, 2008; Feldman, Eidelman, & Rotenberg, 2004).

Though much of this evidence is based on observations of mother–child interactions, research indicates the potential impact of nonparental caregivers (i.e., teachers) on infant development. For example, attachment studies indicate that infants can become securely attached to their nonparental caregivers or teachers through interactive and responsive behavior (Bowlby, 2007; Howes & Hamilton, 1992; van IJzendoorn, Sagi, & Lambermon, 1992), and those who do are more likely to be socially competent (Mitchell-Copeland, Denham, & DeMulder, 1997), exhibit higher levels of play (Cassibba, Van IJzendoorn, & D'Odorico, 2000), and explore their environment and develop a sense of independence or autonomy (Howes & Smith, 1995). In addition, as part of the groundbreaking National Institute of Child Health and Human Development Early Child Care Research Network (NICHD ECCRN) Study of Early Child Care, high-quality early child care as measured by observations of responsive teacher behavior predicted better socioemotional and cognitive-linguistic outcomes throughout the first 3 years of life compared to peers enrolled in lower quality child care (NICHD ECCRN, 1996, 2000a, 2000b, 2001, 2003). Furthermore, these positive outcomes persisted to at least 15 years of age (Vandell et al., 2010).

THE CLASS FRAMEWORK

The CLASS Infant is an age-related downward extension of the CLASS Pre-K and Toddler observational assessments of teacher–child interactions in classroom settings (LaParo, Hamre, & Pianta, 2012; Pianta, LaParo, & Hamre, 2008). The development of the CLASS Infant was informed by the extensive research and implementation experience associated with the CLASS Pre-K and Toddler, as well as prior research on developmentally appropriate teacher–child interactions in child care settings serving infants and toddlers (Copple & Bredekamp, 2009; Hamre & Pianta, 2007; NICHD ECCRN, 1996). To remain consistent with previous versions of the CLASS, we use the term *teacher* to refer to any caregiver in a setting providing child care to children between the ages of 6 weeks and 18 months. Classrooms refer to settings ranging from more formal center-based care to informal care provided in homes and family child care settings in which the adult observed may actually be a parent of one or more of the children present.

An underlying assumption of the theoretical and measurement framework informing the several versions of the CLASS (i.e., Infant, Toddler, Pre-K, K–3) is heterotypic continuity in effective teacher–child interactions across varying age levels. In this use, *heterotypic continuity* refers to the underlying similarity and significance for children's development of features of teacher–child interaction across varying ages, even when the specific examples or behaviors indicating those features may be different for different-age children. More specifically, this means that the dimensions used in the CLASS to define and assess effective teacher–child interactions are similar across the infant, toddler, and preschool periods. The behaviors of teachers that indicate these dimensions, however, are specific to particular developmental levels or age groups (i.e., infant versus toddler; toddler versus preschool). In other words, although Teacher Sensitivity is a critical dimension of effective teacher–child interaction having value for preschoolers or for infants, the specific behaviors through which Teacher Sensitivity may be demonstrated in practice may differ across ages. As another example, the types of language exchanges between teachers and infants or toddlers or preschoolers may vary with regard to their value for promoting language development, and thus, the behaviors teachers engage in to support developing language may be different across these ages. In most cases of aligning CLASS dimensions across ages or developmental periods, the name of the dimension remains the same (e.g., Teacher Sensitivity); however, for the CLASS Infant, the data and theoretical support suggested some nomenclature shifts in names of dimensions. For example, CLASS Infant describes interactions that promote language development in terms of the dimension of Early Language Support, whereas the Toddler and Pre-K manuals describe this feature of interaction using the dimension of Language Modeling.

By providing a common language for discussion of effective teaching across age levels, the CLASS framework attempts to address the need for continuity and coherence in education while providing a context-specific and developmentally sensitive metric for each age level (Bogard & Takanishi, 2005; Essa, Favre, & Thweatt, 1999; Howes, Hamilton, & Philipsen, 1998). In attempting to create a developmentally sensitive metric for each age level, it is important to acknowledge that teacher–infant interactions are inherently different from those of older children and teachers. This can be attributed, in part, to teacher–infant interactions often occurring during routine care and to the dependency of infants on adults.

THE CLASS INFANT DIMENSIONS

The CLASS Infant consists of four theory-based dimensions of teacher–infant interaction: Relational Climate, Teacher Sensitivity, Facilitated Exploration, and Early Language Support. As an indicator of overall quality of teacher–infant interaction in settings providing infant care, these four dimensions are averaged to form a composite referred to as Responsive Caregiving. This section provides summary information on the CLASS Infant dimensions, with more scoring detail provided in Chapter 3.

Relational Climate

The dimension of Relational Climate reflects the quality of relationships between caregivers and children, emotional warmth, and indicators of respect and perspective-taking conveyed by teachers in the context of infants' responses to these interactions. The Relational Climate dimension consists of four indicators:

- *Relational behaviors:* Reflects the consistency of positive behaviors, physical closeness, sharing attention, and the degree of affection shown toward infants

- *Emotion expression:* Captures the extent of smiling and laughter from teachers as well as general happiness and playfulness of infants

- *Respect for infants' state:* Encompasses the degree to which teachers' interactions with infants are calm, gentle, respectful, and informative

- *Lack of adult negativity:* Reflects the absence of negativity, irritability, frustration, or rough behavior on the part of teachers

Teacher Sensitivity

The dimension of Teacher Sensitivity encompasses teachers' awareness of and responsiveness to infants' verbal and nonverbal cues, including availability to provide comfort, skill in resolving distress, and timeliness and contingency of responses. The Teacher Sensitivity dimension consists of three indicators:

- *Awareness and cue detection:* Reflects the consistency of teachers' attention to and awareness of infants

- *Responsiveness:* Captures the teachers' response to the individual needs of infants

- *Infant comfort*: Encompasses the general level of infants' contentment and degree to which infants seek out teachers when upset or happy

Facilitated Exploration

The dimension of Facilitated Exploration considers teachers' involvement with infants, their facilitation of experiences, and their interactions in routine care and playtime to support infants' engagement and development. The Facilitated Exploration dimension consists of three indicators:

- *Involvement:* Reflects the extent to which teachers are actively involved with infants and take part in play and routines

- *Infant focused:* Assesses the consistency of infant-focused behavior by teachers and whether exploration opportunities are provided

- *Expansion of infants' experience:* Captures teachers' efforts to add to infants' experience through physical and verbal encouragement and adjustment of activities

Early Language Support

The dimension of Early Language Support captures the amount and effectiveness of teachers' use of language-stimulation and language-facilitation techniques to encourage infants' early language development. The Early Language Support dimension consists of three indicators:

- *Teacher talk:* Reflects the consistency with which teachers provide language in the classroom

- *Communication support:* Captures teachers' initiation and/or repetition of sounds in direct interactions with infants

- *Communication extension:* Encompasses teachers' efforts to extend communication attempts by adding words to actions and sounds and modeling turn-taking

Observing Infant Settings Using the CLASS

This chapter describes the recommended procedures for using the Classroom Assessment Scoring System® (CLASS®) Infant in classroom observations. These procedures may be adapted to fit the specific needs of a program or intended use, but any adaptation(s) should keep the following principles in mind:

- This tool is primarily intended for use in classrooms serving children 15 months or younger but can be used in classrooms serving children up to 18 months old.

- Maximizing the number of observations will increase the reliability of aggregate scores, and it is recommended that at least four observation cycles be obtained.

- It is important to observe during both structured and unstructured times of the day and across a range of activities so that obtained scores are reflective of the general properties of teacher–infant interaction.

- Observations can and should be carried out during routine care times such as feeding, diapering, and putting infants down for a nap.

Unlike discrete behavioral coding, the CLASS tool requires the observer to use judgment to derive one rating for each dimension per observation cycle, based on the degree to which certain behavioral markers characterize the classroom during that cycle. Behavioral examples are provided in Chapter 3 to assist the coder in making a judgment about the rating, but it is important to note that not all the behaviors are required for a dimension to be assigned a high score. A rating ranging from 1 (*minimally characteristic*) to 7 (*highly characteristic*) is assigned for each dimension and represents the extent to which that dimension is characteristic of teacher–infant interaction in that cycle. To assign ratings, the observer must make judgments based on the depth, frequency, and duration of interactions during the observation time.

CLASS TRAINING

It is important to note that all users must obtain adequate training before attempting to use the CLASS. The CLASS is a multifaceted observation system that requires in-depth training for appropriate use. The level of training depends on the intended use of the system. Attendance at official training workshops is essential for all individuals interested in using the CLASS to collect standardized data on classrooms or for research, accountability, or evaluation purposes. Many options are available for training on the CLASS. To obtain more information on training, please visit http://www.teachstone.org.

If the CLASS is being used for research or evaluative purposes, it is also important that regular checks on reliability occur after initial training. Conducting regular "double-coding" sessions during which at least two observers code the same classroom observations and check their coders for consistency is highly recommended. In addition, holding regular meetings during which observers review video segments together can help keep coding consistent. Finally, it is recommended that all observers watch several refresher/drift segments at least once per year after training or prior to each data collection wave to ensure a high degree of reliability with the manual and master codes.

GENERAL LIVE OBSERVATION PROCEDURES

CLASS observation typically starts at the beginning of the day and continues throughout the morning. However, the observation can be scheduled to begin later in the day, as desired by individual programs. Prior to the observation, the observer should discuss with the teacher the schedule for the day and use that information to plan the observation so as to maximize the number of observation cycles that can be obtained.

CLASS observation procedures require observers to watch, without interruption, activities in the classroom and/or outside for 15 minutes. This 15-minute observation period is called a *cycle,* and it is the source of information that will determine codes or ratings assigned for the CLASS dimensions. During an observation cycle, observers attend carefully to teachers' interactions and behaviors with infants, particularly those that correspond to the CLASS Infant dimensions and behavioral indicators. Notes must be taken for each dimension and corresponding indicators during every observation cycle. These notes form the basis for ratings. Notes should reflect the behavioral indicators of the dimension and not contain extraneous information. Notetaking typically helps observers focus on key aspects of the interaction they are watching.

At the end of the 15 minutes of dedicated observation and notetaking, observers then derive and assign numerical ratings for each of the CLASS dimensions. These ratings are based on observers' knowledge of the dimension definitions and behavioral markers and the written notes that observers recorded during the entire observation cycle for each dimension. More detail about scoring will follow at the end of this chapter. After assigning ratings, observers should begin a new CLASS observation cycle.

Classroom Settings for Infants

Throughout this manual, the term *classroom* is used to refer to the settings infants are observed in. Infants, however, spend their out-of-home care in a variety of settings, ranging from center-based classrooms to neighborhood child care settings. Though most of the development and piloting of CLASS Infant occurred in center-based infant classrooms, the tool can be used successfully in other settings as well. The most common issues observers experience both in center-based classrooms and neighborhood settings are addressed in more detail in the following subsections. It is recommended that tool users visit the intended settings prior to observations to consider the unique features and challenges that might be associated with the setting.

Mixed-Age Classrooms

In some settings and classrooms, the age range of children varies, making it unclear what version of CLASS is best to use. Depending on the needs of the project, different options can be used to address this. In some cases, the best decision may be to use the tool associated with the age range of the majority of the children observed. For example, if the majority of children are younger than 1 year old but there are also a couple of 18-month-olds, CLASS Infant would be the recommended tool to use. Similarly, if the majority of the classroom includes 18-month-olds with one or two 1-year-olds, CLASS Toddler would be the recommended tool to use. In other situations, the project needs might be better met by rotating between two CLASS versions. For example, if the classroom consists of half the children younger than 1 year old and half the children around 2 years old, the project could rotate observation cycles between using CLASS Toddler and CLASS Infant. This decision will provide important information regarding the quality of the teacher–infant interactions observed, but the data will need to be compiled and shared slightly differently.

Settings with More than One Teacher or Adult

The vast majority of infant settings will have more than one teacher in them, so an observer will need to weigh the teachers' behaviors according to the number of infants with whom they are working, the amount of time they spend with the infants, and their responsibility for the activities.

The CLASS dimensions are intended to reflect the effectiveness of interactions for all of the infants in the setting or, in other words, the experience of a typical or average infant in the setting. The dimensions do not target a single infant or a single adult but instead are intended to capture the interactions available to all infants in the setting. When more than one adult is present in a setting, observers must be clear about how to weigh the contributions of each adult when they assign scores on the CLASS dimensions.

Observers must use their judgment to decide how to balance their observation time and the resulting codes. Again, the primary principle to remember is that the CLASS ratings should reflect the experiences of the typical or average infant in the setting. If small groups of infants are participating in separate activities (e.g., diapering, feeding, playing) and a separate adult is working with each group, the observer should spend time watching each group and should code the average of these experiences over the whole 15 minutes, across the groups. If the second adult is merely monitoring infants in the group while another adult is leading, the codes should be based primarily on the behaviors of the adult leading the activity. If an adult has complete responsibility for the infants and activities for a period of time while the other adult prepares food or gathers materials, the observer should code according to what the primary adult is doing.

Rules for What to Observe and Terminating a Cycle

Ratings are based on the interactions and activities of children who are awake during the observation. For the most part, observers should watch and code nearly all of the activities that take place in the classroom. Observers may follow the infants and teachers outside. Observers should code during routine care activities during the day, such as diapering, feeding (bottle or food), and preparing for nap time.

If there is an unexpected disruption in the classroom, such as a fire drill or sudden illness of the teacher, the observer should stop observing. Ratings can still be assigned to the CLASS dimensions based on what the observer has seen up to that point, provided that a minimum of 10 minutes of the observation have been completed. The ratings will be based on what was observed during that 10-minute period.

If the observation cycle is terminated before 10 minutes of observation have occurred, the next observation period should be started once the activity fits the eligible observation description described previously. For example, if the infants return from a shift in settings (e.g., going outside, coming back inside), observation can begin during the transition. It is fine, and in fact desirable, to observe during the transition between these activities.

Challenges for the Observer

The CLASS requires observers to make a series of judgments. Although very detailed behavioral markers in the manual and CLASS observation training help guide this judgment, observers should keep in mind several important challenges while using the CLASS. These challenges are discussed in more detail in the following subsections.

Remaining Objective

Over the course of a complete visit, observers must guard against injecting external explanations for what they see taking place within the classroom. The observer must remain true to the individual dimensions. For example, the observer may be tempted to make allowances for the time of day. Thoughts such as "The teacher must be tired, considering she has all these crying and clinging babies" must not be considered in coding. The dimension and its markers remain stable. The numerical ratings change based on behaviors observed. When assigning scores, it is imperative to base codes on the written descriptions of the dimensions.

Observers should not adjust their codes upward or downward based on any information other than what they have observed in the classroom. It is a common inclination to inflate ratings because observers take the perspective of the teacher: "Oh, she didn't really mean to do that. She just didn't see who really was at fault." "He would have provided a better activity, if there were more balls for the infants. I've had things like that happen lots of times." "He didn't really mean to be so negative. He was just frustrated." Perspective-taking such as this may cause the observer to adjust the codes to explain more positively what takes place at any given time in the classroom. Such perspective-taking should be minimized as much as possible. In addition, the observer should be careful not to adjust ratings based solely on the activity provided for the infants. For example, if the teacher is quietly changing an infant's diaper and makes one good communication extension related to Early Language Support, the coder should not adjust the score significantly higher for this because "She could only do so much since she had to change the infant's diaper." The descriptions of dimensions in the manual should always be the basis for assigning scores.

Another area in which observers must be careful to remain objective is in the tendency to develop initial impressions of teachers and to look for evidence confirming these initial impressions. This tendency often causes observers to miss important behaviors that may disconfirm these initial impressions. It is sometimes helpful for observers to consciously reflect on their initial impressions a few minutes into the observation and then make an active effort to look for disconfirming evidence. In addition, while observers are reviewing notes prior to scoring—particularly if all of their notes reflect one end of the dimension—they should spend a minute reading through the other end of the dimension to see if that cues any thoughts about behaviors they may have seen but failed to record.

Independence of Cycles

Another challenge for the observer is to record the ratings accurately without regard to how each dimension was scored in previous cycles. Each cycle must be considered independently of the others, with no expectation or need for change or stability. Any pattern in the ratings across time should occur naturally and must be external to the observer's manipulation. For example, there may be little change within one activity or across activities with the same teacher in the same classroom. The observer may sense that he or she is responsible for this apparent redundancy or even that, at times, he or she is just giving the same ratings over and over again. There is no expectation, however, that the ratings must vary or remain stable from cycle to cycle to be considered accurate or to document that the observer is not in what might appear to be a response bias.

Weighing Single Incidents

Care should be taken not to allow a single incident to be given too much weight in an overall rating. In general, specific incidents that are markers for the different dimensions should be noted and contribute to the rating, but care should be taken that the rating characterizes the whole observation period and not a single occurrence. Observers should make sure that they mentally review the entire observation segment prior to giving a rating.

Exemplars

For each rating category (i.e., high, mid, and low) on all of the dimensions, examples are included in the form of statements. Remember that these are only examples, and everything in the example does not have to be true in order for a classroom to fit into a given rating category. In addition, events and situations that occur in classrooms may not be included in the examples, but still fit well within a given rating category for a given dimension. The examples are intended to serve as guidelines but are not an exhaustive list of all behaviors that could fit into a rating category.

Independence of Dimensions

The dimensions are intended to be analytically distinct, although overlap occurs. It is often the case that an individual incident in a classroom contributes to the scoring on several dimensions; however, each dimension still should be rated independently.

Seeking Perfection

The high-end markers for each dimension reflect good teaching practice; however, to score in the high range, a classroom does not have to be perfect. Though there may be one or two things that are less than ideal in a given observation, if the overall classroom experience is characterized by the markers at the high end, then the classroom should be scored that way. This may be an issue for observers using the CLASS tool as a professional development tool. Receiving a high score on a dimension does not preclude the usefulness of a discussion with the teacher being observed about his or her practice in that area. It is often the case that teachers are not aware of exactly what they are doing well; hearing the specifics of their successes might help them to be more intentional and consistent in implementing these practices in the future.

SCORING WITH THE CLASS TOOL

Scoring with the CLASS results in a set of scores for each classroom representing quality as observed on each dimension during each observation cycle. These scores can be averaged across cycles and consolidated to create a Responsive Caregiving domain score.

Scoring within Each Cycle

CLASS scoring should be completed immediately after each observation cycle using the observation sheet (see Figure 2.1); that is, it is not standardized procedure to take notes and assign ratings at some period other than immediately after the observation window (e.g., to return to the office and assign ratings based on notes). Before ratings are assigned, the observer should carefully review the CLASS Dimensions Overview for each dimension (e.g., Relational Climate, Teacher Sensitivity) to make initial decisions about the extent to which the observed behaviors reflect a low-, mid-, or high-range score. Then, observers

OBSERVATION SHEET

School: __C-22__   Classroom: __1__
Teacher: __601__   Observer: __522__
Date: __September 1__   Cycle: __1__
Start time: __8:00 am__   End time: __8:15 am__
Double? __ Yes √ No

ACTIVITY SETTING (circle all that occur; check primary)	PHYSICAL SETTING (circle all that occur; check primary)	NUMBER PRESENT: (count number in room at end of cycle)
(Napping)	(√ Classroom)	Adults: __2__
__ Feeding	__ Outside	Primary language English? √ Yes __ No
(√ Play)	__ Other: _____	Total children: __5__ Asleep: __2__ Awake: __3__
__ Diapering		Of those awake: Walkers: ____ Nonwalkers: __3__
__ Other: _____		

Circle appropriate score

Relational Climate (RC) • Relational behaviors • Emotion expression • Respect for infants' state • Lack of adult negativity	*Notes:* · Affection → teacher pats Ellie on back, foot · Teacher often smiles at the infants · Communicates intentions → "I'm gonna help you up"	1 2 3 4 5 6 ⑦
Teacher Sensitivity (TS) • Awareness and cue detection • Responsiveness • Infant comfort	*Notes:* · Teacher notices when infants are ready for another bite · Acknowledges emotions → "Are you excited?" "I can see that you're upset" · Infants soothed by teacher → Allison stops crying when picked up	1 2 3 4 5 6 ⑦
Facilitated Exploration (FE) • Involvement • Infant focused • Expansion of infants' experience	*Notes:* · Teacher mirrors behavior → sways with Miles, shakes maraca · Takes scarf from Allison before she is done · Adjusts experience by getting out scarves, books	1 2 3 4 5 ⑥ 7
Early Language Support (ELS) • Teacher talk • Communication support • Communication extension	*Notes:* · Teacher sometimes describes classroom events → "Miles, you're waving your arms" · Occasionally imitates sounds → "ba ba ba" · Provides words for infants' communication → "You're looking at the book" "Are you saying hi?"	1 2 3 4 ⑤ 6 7

Figure 2.1. Filled-in CLASS® Infant Observation Sheet.

Table 2.1. Scoring guidelines for the Classroom Assessment Scoring System® (CLASS®) Infant tool

Low range		Mid-range			High range	
1	2	3	4	5	6	7
The low-range description fits the classroom and/or teacher very well. All, or almost all, relevant indicators in the low range are present.	The low-range description mostly fits the classroom and/or teacher, but there are one or two indicators in the mid-range.	The mid-range description mostly fits the classroom and/or teacher, but there are one or two indicators in the low range.	The mid-range description fits the classroom and/or teacher very well. All, or almost all, relevant indicators in the mid-range are present.	The mid-range description mostly fits the classroom and/or teacher, but there are one or two indicators in the high range.	The high-range description mostly fits the classroom and/or teacher, but there are one or two indicators in the mid-range.	The high-range description fits the classroom and/or teacher very well. All, or almost all, relevant indicators in the high range are present.

should read the more detailed description of the scores in the manual to finalize their rating. *Because assigning accurate scores using CLASS requires judgment, ratings should not be assigned without referring to the manual.*

It is important to note that although the manual provides a general scoring guideline, *the CLASS is not a checklist,* and observers should view the dimensions as reflecting low-, mid-, and high-range holistic descriptions of teacher–infant interaction. More important, it is not necessary that all examples of various behavioral markers fall within the same range of low, mid, or high to assign a score. After a thorough review of observation notes and the manual, observers use judgment to assign a score for each dimension using the 7-point range outlined in the manual (see Table 2.1). The dimension descriptions provide a thorough explanation of each scale at the low (1, 2), mid (3, 4, 5), and high (6, 7) ranges.

Getting Composite Scores Across Cycles

To get composite scores across cycles, individual cycle scores are averaged across the number of cycles of observations completed. For example, the sample Scoring Summary Sheet in Figure 2.2 contains cycle-level scores from six observation cycles. Scores for each dimension are averaged, and the average score is recorded in the last column of the Scoring Summary Sheet. On the sample Scoring Summary Sheet, Relational Climate was scored as a 7, 6, 7, 5, 6, and 6 across the six cycles. Summing these scores and dividing by the number of cycles (6) yields the average Relational Climate domain score of 6.17 recorded in the final column of the table. Continue down the column, averaging scores within each dimension across all observation cycles.

Obtaining the Responsive Caregiving Domain Score

Once all of the average dimension scores are obtained, the Responsive Caregiving domain score can be calculated. This domain score represents the average of each of the corresponding dimension scores (following the formula provided; see Figure 2.2). Average dimension scores are transferred to the corresponding spaces in the domain score box on the right side of the Scoring Summary Sheet. Calculate the average of the dimension scores and enter it in the space provided. In Figure 2.2, the sum of the average dimension scores is divided by 4, and the Responsive Caregiving domain score is calculated as 5.71.

SCORING SUMMARY SHEET

School: C-22   Classroom: 1

Teacher: 601   Observer: 522

Start time: 8:00 am   End time: 10:20 am

DIRECTIONS:
Copy scores from observation sheets. Compute average scores for each dimension by adding cycle scores and then dividing by the number of cycles completed.

	Cycle 1	Cycle 2	Cycle 3	Cycle 4	Cycle 5	Cycle 6	Average
Number of children asleep	2	0	0	0	1	1	
Number of children awake	3	5	5	6	5	5	
Number of adults	2	2	2	2	2	2	
Activity (circle all that occur; check primary)	(Napping) / Feeding / ✓Play / Diapering / Other: ___	Napping / ✓(Feeding) / Play / Diapering / Other: ___	Napping / Feeding / Play / ✓(Diapering) / Other: ___	Napping / Feeding / ✓(Play) / Diapering / Other: ___	(Napping) / Feeding / ✓(Play) / Diapering / Other: ___	(Napping) / Feeding / ✓(Play) / Diapering / Other: ___	
Physical setting (circle all that occur; check primary)	(Classroom) / Outside / Other: ___	(Classroom) / Outside / Other: ___	(Classroom) / Outside / Other: ___	Classroom / (Outside) / Other: ___	(Classroom) / Outside / Other: ___	(Classroom) / Outside / Other: ___	
Start time	8:00	8:25	8:50	9:15	9:40	10:05	
End time	8:15	8:40	9:05	9:30	9:55	10:20	
RC	1 2 3 4 5 6 (7)	1 2 3 4 5 (6) 7	1 2 3 4 5 6 (7)	1 2 3 4 (5) 6 7	1 2 3 4 5 (6) 7	1 2 3 4 5 (6) 7	6.17
TS	1 2 3 4 5 6 (7)	1 2 3 4 5 6 (7)	1 2 3 4 5 6 (7)	1 2 3 4 5 (6) 7	1 2 3 4 5 (6) 7	1 2 3 4 5 (6) 7	6.50
FE	1 2 3 4 5 (6) 7	1 2 3 4 5 (6) 7	1 2 3 4 (5) 6 7	1 2 3 (4) 5 6 7	1 2 3 4 5 (6) 7	1 2 3 4 (5) 6 7	5.33
ELS	1 2 3 4 (5) 6 7	1 2 3 (4) 5 6 7	1 2 3 4 (5) 6 7	1 2 3 4 5 (6) 7	1 2 3 4 5 (6) 7	1 2 (3) 4 5 6 7	4.83

Responsive Caregiving

$$\frac{6.17}{RC} + \frac{6.50}{TS} + \frac{5.33}{FE} + \frac{4.83}{ELS} \; / \; 4 = \boxed{5.71}$$

Figure 2.2. Filled-in CLASS® Infant Scoring Summary Sheet.

CLASS Infant Dimensions

CHAPTER THREE

Taken together, the four Classroom Assessment Scoring System® (CLASS®) Infant dimensions represent one domain—Responsive Caregiving. The four dimensions are

- Relational Climate

- Teacher Sensitivity

- Facilitated Exploration

- Early Language Support

This chapter provides information on each of the CLASS dimensions. The section detailing each dimension includes a face page that provides a short overview along with a concise description of the low-, mid-, and high-range indicators for each dimension. The CLASS observer should use these short overview pages to become familiar with the various dimensions, but not for scoring purposes. For scoring purposes, refer to the comprehensive descriptions of the low-, mid-, and high-range indicators provided in this chapter for each dimension.

Users of the CLASS Infant should review this chapter thoroughly. When scoring following an observation, it is helpful to first read each overview page and make an initial judgment about whether the classroom falls in the low, mid, or high range, then turn to the relevant low-, mid-, or high-range description and carefully read that section. If the description does not quite fit, read the other descriptions for that dimension before scoring. Then use the scoring recommendations in Table 2.1 to determine a final score for the dimension. Continue this procedure for all dimensions.

Relational Climate

Reflects the connections, emotions, and respect conveyed by teachers as well as the infants' responses to these interactions.

	Low (1, 2)	Mid (3, 4, 5)	High (6, 7)
Relational behaviors • Proximity • Eye contact • Joint attention • Affection	Teachers and infants seldom appear connected. Teachers rarely are near infants or show physical or verbal affection to them.	Teachers are inconsistent in their behavior with infants. Sometimes they may be close to infants and display verbal or physical affection, but at other times they are disengaged.	Teachers consistently display positive behaviors with infants by being physically close, being on eye level, sharing attention, and providing affection and contact.
Emotion expression • Smiling • Laughing • Enthusiasm	Teachers rarely express positive emotion. Multiple infants cry for extended periods of time. The majority of the infants show negative or no positive emotional response to teachers.	Teachers sometimes smile and laugh but at other times appear flat in their interactions. Infants show periods of happiness but may also show distress or negative emotions.	There are frequent episodes of smiles and laughter by teachers and infants. Teachers and infants generally appear happy in the classroom.
Respect for infants' state • Calm voice • Gentle approach • Communication of intentions, transitions, or changes • Respectful language	Teachers' tone or movements are sudden and often startle or upset infants. Teachers often move infants or change activities without communicating intent. Teachers rarely use infants' names when in proximity to them or to gain their attention.	Teachers are generally calm, respectful, and gentle with infants but at times may be abrupt in tone or actions. Teachers communicate intentions but may also "act on" infants without notifying them first. Sometimes they use respectful language and refer to infants using their names.	Teachers frequently use a calm tone, respectful language, and gentle touch when moving or holding infants. They consistently verbally prepare infants for what is about to happen. They consistently use respectful language and refer to infants using their names.
Lack of adult negativity • Lack of irritation/ frustration • Lack of verbal harshness • Lack of rough handling • Lack of negative comments	Teachers consistently demonstrate harsh voice or touch with infants. Teachers often make comments that are negative or sarcastic either to infants or adults.	Teachers on occasion get agitated with infants. Teachers at times make negative comments or are sarcastic, but this is not characteristic of the way teachers typically talk with infants or others.	There is a clear absence of negativity, irritability, or frustration on the part of the teachers. No roughness with infants is observed.

Low Relational Climate (1, 2)

Teachers and infants seldom appear connected. Teachers rarely are near infants or show physical or verbal affection to them. Teachers and infants do not appear to be connected to one another in any meaningful way. They appear distant and lack genuine interactions with one another. Teachers are physically distant from infants or stand over infants when talking to them. Teachers rarely show physical affection with infants. If teachers talk to the infants, the talk appears to be "at" the infants rather than "with" them. Teachers rarely provide verbal affection or positive statements to infants.

Teachers rarely express positive emotion. Multiple infants cry for extended periods of time. The majority of the infants show negative or no positive emotional response to teachers. There are few instances, if any, of teachers and infants sharing positive emotions. When the infants are smiling or laughing, teachers rarely smile or laugh back. Teachers' affect appears consistently flat, with only very rare occasions of smiling or laughter. There are frequent time periods when infants are crying. Teachers often appear to be just going through the motions of teaching or interacting with the infants. Teachers show little, if any, enthusiasm, or they speak in a monotone voice.

Teachers' tones or movements are sudden and often startle or upset infants. Teachers often move infants or change activities without communicating intent. Teachers rarely use infants' names when in proximity to them or to gain their attention. Teachers rarely use a warm, calm voice when talking with infants. Teachers often pick up infants or physically manipulate them (e.g., to check their diapers or wipe their faces) without first giving them verbal indication of what they are about to do. Teachers rarely use respectful words (e.g., "thank you," "please"). Teachers infrequently address infants by their names or regularly call them by incorrect names.

Teachers consistently demonstrate harsh voice or touch with infants. Teachers often make comments that are negative or sarcastic either to infants or adults. Teachers regularly appear irritated during interactions with infants or during routine care. For example, they show signs of frustration by rolling their eyes and saying, "You made a mess again!" when an infant spits up. Teachers get visibly agitated at an infant who continues to cry over an extended period of time. For example, they may say, "There's nothing wrong; quit crying!" and place the infant in a crib, or make a more rhetorical comment, such as "I told your mother that this formula made you sick." Teachers occasionally are rough in their touch, such as pulling infants up by their arms or pushing them away. If interactions between adults do occur, they may be flat, sarcastic, and/or include negative affect, and/or the content of the interactions may be negative either about them or the children.

Note: Peer-to-peer negativity is not considered in the score, but how the teacher responds to the negativity does count toward the score.

Mid-Range Relational Climate (3, 4, 5)

Teachers are inconsistent in their behavior with infants. Sometimes they may be close to infants and display verbal or physical affection, but at other times they are disengaged. Teachers generally appear to be positive in interactions, but at times or with certain infants there is a constrained element to interactions. Teachers are regularly in close proximity to infants, but they do not consistently interact with them. For example, a teacher watches infants but is focused and talking to another adult or is disengaged from the current activity. Teachers at this level occasionally provide physical affection by giving hugs or rubbing infants' backs or give verbal affection by commenting on their feelings toward the infants. Teachers sometimes engage in joint attention with infants by following their gaze, getting on the same level, and/or joining them in their activities.

Teachers sometimes smile and laugh but at other times appear flat in their interactions. Infants show periods of happiness but may also show distress or negative emotions. Teachers display positive affect but only with some infants or some of the time. Teachers laugh and smile during some activities but appear flat during others. At times, teachers and infants laugh or smile together. There may be periods of infants crying, but they are short lived. Infants at times laugh or gurgle with teachers, visually track them when they leave, or provide other indications that they are happy or content.

Teachers are generally calm, respectful, and gentle with infants but at times may be abrupt in tone or actions. Teachers communicate intentions but may also "act on" infants without notifying them first. Sometimes they use respectful language and refer to infants using their names. Sometimes teachers speak with a warm and calm voice. At times, teachers communicate intentions to infants before physically moving them or acting upon them (e.g., wiping their noses or faces). Teachers talk to infants with their back turned to them or when they do not have their attention. Teachers occasionally use words that show respect, such as "please" and "thank you." Teachers sometimes use infants' names during interactions or to get their attention, but at other times the infants are not addressed by name.

Teachers on occasion get agitated with infants. Teachers at times make negative comments or are sarcastic, but this is not characteristic of the way teachers typically talk with infants or others. Teachers at times use an agitated tone, either with infants or adults, but the tone does not persist in the interactions. For example, a teacher shows mild irritation when she discovers that an infant needs a diaper change but alters her tone during the routine so the irritation is no longer present. Or, a teacher briefly expresses agitation when an infant drops his bottle causing a large spill, but during the cleanup says to the infant, "It's all right; accidents happen." Overall, teachers are not negative when interacting with infants and adults, but there may be some brief observed expressions of negativity.

High Relational Climate (6, 7)

Teachers consistently display positive behaviors with infants by being physically close, being on eye level, sharing attention, and providing affection and contact. Teachers and infants show clear evidence that they enjoy being with one another. Teachers are often in physical proximity to infants, sitting next to them on their level, such as on the floor or at the table. Teachers often touch, hug, or pat infants and make comments such as "Lucy, I am so glad you are here," or "Tomas, we are so happy to see you!" Throughout these interactions, teachers regularly look at infants, are on their level, join in their activities, and share verbal and physical affection.

There are frequent episodes of smiles and laughter by teachers and infants. Teachers and infants generally appear happy in the classroom. Teachers exhibit a consistent display of enthusiasm, including laughter or smiling. There is a match between teachers' and infants' positive affect, such that when the infants show excitement and enthusiasm, so do teachers. For instance, when an infant laughs while ripping wax paper, teachers share the joy back. There may be brief moments of infants crying, but the general emotion displayed in the classroom is positive.

Teachers frequently use a calm tone, respectful language, and gentle touch when moving or holding infants. They consistently verbally prepare infants for what is about to happen. They consistently use respectful language and refer to infants using their names. Teachers consistently use a warm and calm voice. They regularly say what they are about to do with an infant prior to doing it. For example, when needing to move infants physically, such as picking them up for a diaper change, checking their diapers, or wiping their noses, teachers explain what they are going to do before physically moving or touching them. Teachers regularly use infants' names and language that communicates respect, such as "please" and "thank you."

There is a clear absence of negativity, irritability, or frustration on the part of the teachers. No roughness with infants is observed. Teachers rarely, if ever, show negativity in their interactions with infants and other adults. For example, if an infant is upset for an extended period of time, teachers do not display any negativity or irritation while trying to soothe him. Teachers do not display negativity or disdain for anyone in the classroom. If exchanges between teachers or other adults occur, they are informative or positive.

Teacher Sensitivity

Encompasses teachers' awareness of and responsiveness to infants' verbal and nonverbal cues, including availability to provide comfort, skill in resolving distress, and timeliness and contingency of responses.

	Low (1, 2)	Mid (3, 4, 5)	High (6, 7)
Awareness and cue detection • Visually scan • Attend physically • Acknowledge verbally and/or physically	Teachers are inattentive to most infants in the classroom. There is little verbal or physical acknowledgment of cues.	Teachers sometimes show awareness of infants in the room through looking around but at other times fail to notice or acknowledge cues.	Teachers consistently physically orient toward the majority of the infants and regularly look around the room. Teachers continuously acknowledge infants, whether or not they are making bids for attention, by talking to them or giving them a nod or smile.
Responsiveness • Respond to infants' emotions and needs • Adjust actions based on individual needs of the infants	Teachers rarely respond to infants, or they appear to ignore individual signals for attention, comfort, and support.	At times, teachers respond to infants' needs or bids for attention, but at other times the infants' needs for attention, comfort, or support are dismissed or ignored.	Teachers consistently respond to the verbal and physical cues of infants. Teachers adjust responses to meet the individual needs of infants.
Infant comfort • Infants comfortable or content when teachers are present • Infants seek out teachers • Infants soothed or calmed by teachers' efforts	Infants rarely visually or physically seek out teachers and show a general level of discomfort in the classroom. Teachers' attempts to soothe the infant are ineffective or worsen the situation.	Some infants generally appear comfortable with teachers. Infants occasionally seek out teachers or are comforted by their efforts. At other times, teachers' presence or efforts do not calm or soothe the infants.	Infants appear content in the classroom and comfortable with the teachers. Infants look for teachers to acknowledge them when they do something new. Infants look for teachers when upset and are calmed by teachers' presence or soothing efforts.

Low Teacher Sensitivity (1, 2)

Teachers are inattentive to most infants in the classroom. There is little verbal or physical acknowledgment of cues. Teachers are mostly inattentive to the infants, and an infant may have to wait a very long time for the teacher to attend to him or her after making a verbal or nonverbal bid. Teachers leave infants under play structures or in bouncy chairs for an extended period of time without any acknowledgment. Teachers do not appear aware of infants' involvement or lack of involvement in activities and/or tasks. For example, teachers do not regularly scan the room. Or, teachers rarely orient their body position to be able to see the majority of infants.

Teachers rarely respond to infants, or they appear to ignore individual signals for attention, comfort, and support. When infants approach teachers or indicate a need to the teachers, the teachers typically are unresponsive or ignore the request. Teachers do not typically acknowledge infants' emotional expressions. When infants are upset, teachers' responses do not match the seriousness of the situation. For example, the teachers may laugh or smile without validating an infant's feelings. Similarly, when infants are distressed, teachers fail to either recognize this or address their concerns. They do not allow infants to withdraw from the situation and find a quiet area or help them move to another area or activity to assist in calming them. If infants express frustration or confusion, teachers ignore them, "shush" them, or quickly dismiss their problems. Teachers do not shift response styles to meet the individual needs of infants. For example, they may not adjust actions or techniques to calm an upset infant.

Infants rarely visually or physically seek out teachers and show a general level of discomfort in the classroom. Teachers' attempts to soothe the infant are ineffective or worsen the situation. Infants withdraw from teachers. For instance, a crying infant turns his head away from a teacher when approached. Infants rarely seek out teachers for comfort physically, visually, or verbally when they are having a hard time or do not appear comforted by teachers when upset. For example, an infant falls and is crying and does not look for the teachers for comfort. Alternately, a teacher picks up a crying infant but cannot soothe him or her.

Mid-Range Teacher Sensitivity (3, 4, 5)

Teachers sometimes show awareness of infants in the room through looking around but at other times fail to notice or acknowledge cues. At times, teachers are inattentive to the infants, or infants may sometimes have to wait a long time for teachers to attend to them after making a bid for attention. Teachers mostly physically orient toward the infants, but there are times when teachers are not aware of what infants are doing. Teachers sometimes call out to infants to let them know they are there and aware of the infants before physically moving toward the infant, but at other times teachers do not actively acknowledge the infants. Teachers show awareness of infants making bids for attention but fail to acknowledge those not making bids.

At times, teachers respond to infants' needs or bids for attention, but at other times the infants' needs for attention, comfort, or support are dismissed or ignored. Teachers are usually responsive to infants' bids but at times ignore their needs. When there is a lot of activity in the classroom or several infants are requesting attention, some infants' needs are missed. For example, a teacher attends to an infant who needs a diaper change in a timely manner but then is slow to respond to an infant who is upset in the corner of the room. Teachers inconsistently assist infants with their emotions and affective states. For example, the teacher responds to an infant's emotions by saying, "I see that you are upset," but then dismisses the infant by saying, "There's really nothing to be upset about! Go play." Teachers occasionally adjust their response strategies to comfort infants, but at other times they persist with a strategy that is not working.

Some infants generally appear comfortable with the teachers. Infants occasionally seek out teachers or are comforted by their efforts. At other times, teachers' presence or efforts do not calm or soothe the infants. In general, infants appear comfortable and content. At times, infants look to the teachers to share an accomplishment or experience, but this is not typical. When upset, some infants seek out teachers for comfort or reassurance, but others do not. Even after a teacher attempts to soothe infants, the infants may remain weepy or disengaged from an activity for a while.

High Teacher Sensitivity (6, 7)

Teachers consistently physically orient toward the majority of the infants and regularly look around the room. Teachers continuously acknowledge infants, whether or not they are making bids for attention, by talking to them or giving them a nod or smile. Teachers are consistently aware of all infants and areas in the classroom. Almost every time an infant sends verbal or behavioral signals indicating a need for help or attention, teachers notice. Teachers regularly show awareness of infants through verbally addressing those who are not nearby or using nonverbal actions such as smiling at infants when scanning the room. Teachers notice both infants who are making bids for attention as well as those who are not. For example, while a teacher gives a bottle to a crying infant, the teacher positions him- or herself to see the other infants.

Teachers consistently respond to the verbal and physical cues of infants. Teachers adjust responses to meet the individual needs of infants. Teachers respond to infants' needs in a timely manner. For example, after changing one infant's diaper, a teacher checks in with another to see if he or she is ready to eat or wants to play with a new toy. Teachers regularly shift response styles in ways that are consistent with the needs of each infant. For example, a teacher bounces a fussy infant, but when that does not seem to be working, the teacher changes to calm rocking and singing. If an infant is having difficulty, teachers respond in a soothing, understanding, and individualized way. For example, when an infant is upset, the teacher says, "I can see that you are sad or angry" to validate the emotional expression and then looks for a way to calm or distract the infant.

Infants appear content in the classroom and comfortable with the teachers. Infants look for teachers to acknowledge them when they do something new. Infants look for teachers when upset and are calmed by teachers' presence or soothing efforts. Infants look for teachers for support, encouragement, or acknowledgment when they are trying something new. There is little, if any, infant distress. When infants do have problems or are upset, they seek out the teacher physically, visually, or verbally for comfort and guidance, using teachers as a source of support and reassurance. For example, an infant upset by a push from another infant looks for the teacher. A crying infant is quickly calmed by the teacher approaching and leans toward the teacher.

Facilitated Exploration

Considers teachers' facilitation of experiences and interactions in routine care and playtime to support infants' engagement and development.[1]

	Low (1, 2)	Mid (3, 4, 5)	High (6, 7)
Involvement • Initiate interactions • Join in experiences • Mirror behavior	Teachers rarely are in close proximity to infants or mostly passively watch them without interacting. During routines, teachers are minimally involved with infants beyond getting the task done.	Teachers occasionally engage with infants, mirror their behavior, or join in their play but at other times only passively observe infants.	Teachers spend most of their time actively involved with infants, consistently initiating, joining, or mirroring interactions with infants during play and within routines.
Infant focused • Follow infants' leads • Allow infants choice • Support exploration	Teachers' interests dominate infants' activities, or teachers are overstimulating in interactions and rarely allow infants to explore their surroundings. Conversely, teachers seldom provide structure or direction to encourage exploration.	Teachers at times look to infants to follow their interests but at other times are either controlling or overstimulating in interactions with infants. Teachers allow infants some ability to explore but also limit behavior without clear reason.	Teachers consistently watch infants to see what they are interested in and then follow that lead, either in their comments or by activities they select. Teachers provide opportunities for infants to safely explore and choose options in their surroundings.
Expansion of infants' experience • Encourage behavior • Vary intonation • Adjust experience	Teachers rarely adjust, change, or modify experiences to support infants' interests or engagement.	Teachers sometimes say encouraging words, adjust experiences, or provide nonverbal support to encourage infants' involvement or development, but at other times they only passively interact with infants.	Teachers regularly encourage infants to persist in experiences through verbal encouragement and enthusiasm. Teachers often adjust infants' experience to support continued involvement or extend development.

[1]Although all indicators are weighted equally in assigning a code, they are in an intentional order such that they build on one another. For example, teachers typically need to be involved with infants before a coder can consider whether the interaction is infant centered. In addition, teachers need to be centered on the infant before a coder can consider whether the interaction expands the experience. If teachers do not show evidence of involvement with infants, then there likely is also no evidence for the other two indicators. However, all indicators should be considered when looking for evidence and in scoring the dimension.

Low Facilitated Exploration (1, 2)

Teachers rarely are in close proximity to infants or mostly passively watch them without interacting. During routines, teachers are minimally involved with infants beyond getting the task done. Teachers spend most of their time passively monitoring infants or are involved with mostly managerial tasks in the classroom. Teachers typically remain in one area of the classroom, such as in a rocking chair, and do not move around to interact with the infants. Teachers rarely interact with infants on the floor. Teachers hardly ever mirror infants' behavior. For example, when some infants start to wave their arms and legs to music, teachers smile but do not imitate them or join in the interaction. In another example, during diapering, teachers do not mirror an infant who is shaking her head, ignoring the behavior and primarily focusing on completing the routine.

Teachers' interests dominate infants' activities, or teachers are overstimulating in interactions and rarely allow infants to explore their surroundings. Conversely, teachers seldom provide structure or direction to encourage exploration. Teachers regularly show a high degree of control or overstimulation with infants in their movement or activities. Teachers rarely follow infants' leads and rigidly stick to schedules at the expense of infant-initiated interests in activities. For example, even though infants are actively happy and engaged in trying to figure out how to make a ball roll on the floor, a teacher quickly moves them to the kitchen because it is time for lunch. As an example of overstimulation, a teacher pushes a puppet toward an infant's face and makes loud noises such as "woof woof!", and the teacher persists even though the infant keeps turning away and pushing at the puppet in efforts to make it stop. Teachers rarely provide activities or opportunities for infants to independently choose or explore their surroundings. For example, during routines such as feeding, teachers do not allow infants to assist themselves (e.g., hold the spoon). Or, teachers are passive with infants and rarely provide structure or direction with activities, even when infants are not engaged or exploring. For example, infants continue to be left under a mobile or in a bouncy chair even though they no longer show interest in the activity, are looking toward other activities of interest, and/or are physically straining to move out of the chair.

Teachers rarely adjust, change, or modify experiences to support infants' interests or engagement. Teachers rarely change or modify infants' activities or experiences. For example, an infant may be content under a mobile but stays there for an extended period of time without the teacher interacting with or adding to the infant's experience in some way (e.g., singing, adjusting infant's body position to see something new). Teachers rarely provide verbal or nonverbal encouragement to infants. They continue with the same activity even though the infants are unengaged. For example, a teacher continues to read a lengthy book after infants have begun to move away or have started crying, or she continues to shake a rattle in front of an infant even though the infant is reaching to touch or take the rattle.

FACILITATED EXPLORATION

Mid-Range Facilitated Exploration (3, 4, 5)

Teachers occasionally engage with infants, mirror their behavior, or join in their play but at other times only passively observe infants. Teachers move around the room, playing with and talking to infants, but this is not characteristic of the majority of the teachers' involvement. At times, teachers initiate interactions or mirror infants' behavior. For instance, a teacher may see an infant grab two blocks and tap them together, and the teacher then also gets two blocks and taps them together. At other times, however, teachers do not engage with infants.

Teachers at times look to infants to follow their interests but at other times are either controlling or overstimulating in interactions with infants. Teachers allow infants some ability to explore but also limit behavior without clear reason. Teachers occasionally watch to see what infants are interested in and encourage them to explore the objects in the classroom. For example, a teacher and infant are engaged in ball play and the teacher notices that the infant switches attention and turns toward a toy train. The teacher encourages the infant's interest, saying, "Do you like that train? Let's go get it!" At other times, however, teachers limit infants' choices and explorations by not following their leads. For instance, a teacher may see an infant reaching for toys on a shelf but does not take the toys down. Or, during diapering, an infant looks at and reaches for the mobile, but the teacher does not look at the infant or respond. Alternatively, teachers sometimes either are controlling or overstimulating in their actions. For example, a teacher stops an infant from playing with a toy for no clear reason or persists in waving a toy in an infants' face and making loud noises with it even though the infant has turned away and shown that he or she is not comfortable.

Teachers sometimes say encouraging words, adjust experiences, or provide non-verbal support to encourage infants' involvement or development, but at other times only passively interact with infants. Teachers sometimes provide assistance to infants when they are interacting with an object in order to expand the infants' experience. For example, teachers sometimes encourage some infants to reach for objects just out of their grasp or to keep trying to spin a toy, but do not at other times. On occasion, teachers vary their intonation to further encourage an infant to explore or engage. For example, when the teacher sees an infant playing with a lion puppet, the teacher adjusts the tone and uses a "scary" voice, saying, "Oh, this lion is big!" to further engage the infant. Or, during feeding, the teacher moves two infants closer together, expanding their experience by providing an opportunity for peer interactions. At other times, however, teachers do not add to or extend what infants are experiencing.

FACILITATED
EXPLORATION

High Facilitated Exploration (6, 7)

Teachers spend most of their time actively involved with infants, consistently initiating, joining, or mirroring interactions with infants during play and within routines. Teachers regularly move around the room, playing with and talking to the majority of infants. Teachers often join infants in their play or talk with them during feeding and diaper changing. For example, teachers are on the floor shaking toys with infants or making faces back and forth with infants during diapering.

Teachers consistently watch infants to see what they are interested in and then follow that lead, either in their comments or by activities they select. Teachers provide opportunities for infants to safely explore and choose options in their surroundings. Teachers consistently provide choice and encourage exploration around the room and watch infants to see what they are interested in. For instance, the teacher looks over to where the infant is looking and says, "You're looking at the ribbons! Would you like to go over there?" When infants express an interest in a particular toy or game, the teacher follows their lead. For example, when an infant reaches for another infant's rattle, the teacher tells him that there are more and brings out new rattles for him to play with. Teachers also provide adequate time for infants to explore materials and space on their own.

Teachers regularly encourage infants to persist in experiences through verbal encouragement and enthusiasm. Teachers often adjust infants' experience to support continued involvement or extend development. Within play and routines, teachers regularly support infants to continue in or expand upon an experience. Teachers often use verbal encouragement or add an additional element to an interaction to stretch infants' engagement or development. For example, a teacher places an infant's favorite toy a few inches away to encourage crawling, then with an excited tone says, "You can do it!" to further encourage the infant. In another example, the teacher claps and dances to encourage an infant to continue playing with drums. An example of expansion during a routine would include an infant grabbing the teacher's finger during bottle-feeding and the teacher expanding this experience by saying, "This is my finger. It's much bigger than yours!" Teachers expand infants' involvement by encouraging peer interactions in the classroom. For example, a teacher brings out a toy telephone and encourages two infants to talk to each other on the phone.

Early Language Support

Captures the amount and effectiveness of teachers' use of language-stimulation and language-facilitation techniques to encourage infants' early language development.

	Low (1, 2)	Mid (3, 4, 5)	High (6, 7)
Teacher talk • Self-talk • Describe classroom events • Verbally label objects • Use complete and varied sentences	Teachers rarely use words to describe their own or infants' actions or classroom events. Teachers seldom use a variety of words or language structures when talking with infants. There is a noticeable lack of language used in the setting.	Teachers occasionally narrate their own actions during activities or routines or comment to infants on things happening. Teachers sometimes use a variety of novel or descriptive words and language; however, at times there is either a noticeable absence of language or the use of baby talk.	Teachers consistently describe their own and infants' actions during activities and routines. Teachers regularly comment on events happening in the classroom. Teachers' classroom language often includes descriptive and variable words, spoken in complete sentences.
Communication support • Initiate sounds or words • Imitate or repeat sounds	Teachers rarely encourage infants to verbalize by initiating or imitating sounds or words.	Teachers occasionally encourage infants to verbalize by initiating sounds and words with infants or imitating their sounds but at other times remain silent in direct interactions with infants.	Teachers frequently encourage infants to verbalize by initiating sounds and words with infants or imitating sounds expressed by infants.
Communication extension • Provide words for infants' communication • Expand and extend on infants' communication • Model turn-taking	Teachers ignore or rarely respond to infants' communication attempts or engage in verbal exchanges with infants to extend communication.	Teachers sometimes provide words or extend infants' communication attempts but other times do not add language to those attempts. On occasion, teachers engage in back-and-forth verbal exchanges with infants, but this is not typical.	Teachers often extend infants' communication attempts by adding words to actions and sounds. Teachers consistently engage in back-and-forth verbal exchanges with infants, using pauses and eye contact to encourage turn taking.

Low Early Language Support (1, 2)

Teachers rarely use words to describe their own or infants' actions or classroom events. Teachers seldom use a variety of words or language structure when talking with infants. There is a noticeable lack of classroom language used in the setting. There are frequent and extended periods of silence in the setting. Teachers rarely talk in routines or play with infants; teachers seldom describe or verbally map out their actions or map the actions of the infants. When teachers are diapering infants or feeding them, they hardly ever provide any verbal description of what they are doing. Or, during play with infants, they rarely describe or elaborate on what infants are doing. When there is talking, teachers' vocabulary used to explain ideas and objects tends to lack a variety of words or sentence types. For example, teachers use the same few directive words or phrases repeatedly, like "Stop it" or "You're okay." Teachers mostly repeat basic sentences or questions, like "Is it good?" during feedings. Teachers seldom, if ever, verbally label objects. For example, a teacher gives an infant a stuffed animal to play with but does not identify what the animal is.

Teachers rarely encourage infants to verbalize by initiating or imitating sounds or words. Teachers rarely attempt to involve infants by speaking directly to them or responding to them. When infants make verbalizations, teachers hardly ever respond. Teachers seldom repeat infants' communication attempts. For example, a teacher hears an infant say "ba ba" and provides the bottle without verbalizing back. When teachers are interacting with infants, they rarely make sounds or say words to the infants in attempts to have infants produce sounds.

Teachers ignore or rarely respond to infants' communication attempts or engage in verbal exchanges with infants to extend communication. Teachers rarely acknowledge infants' communication attempts. Teachers seldom provide words for infants' vocalizations. If infants are attempting to vocalize using sounds or babbling, teachers rarely expand on the sounds infants are making. For example, if an infant says "ma," the teacher does not expand the sound into "mama" or explain that the infant's mother will be there soon. Teachers rarely, if ever, engage in back-and-forth verbal exchanges with infants. For example, a teacher asks several questions back to back without giving nonverbal cues such as pauses and eye contact to encourage turn taking. Or, infants wave arms or legs or make nonverbal communication attempts, but teachers do not extend the communication attempt by adding language to it through comments or questions.

Mid-Range Early Language Support (3, 4, 5)

Teachers occasionally narrate their own actions during activities or routines or comment to infants on things happening. Teachers sometimes use a variety of novel or descriptive words and language; however, at times there is a noticeable absence of language or the use of baby talk. Teachers sometimes talk during routines and play; they map words to their actions or map words to the actions of some infants. During routines such as diapering or feeding, teachers provide some verbal descriptions of what they are doing, but this happens only with some infants. Teachers sometimes use a variety of vocabulary to explain ideas and objects to some infants. Teachers occasionally use complete and varied sentences in talking in the classroom, but they also use directive words or phrases like "stop now" repeatedly. At times, objects are labeled, but this is inconsistent across the day or only happens with some infants.

Teachers occasionally encourage infants to verbalize by initiating sounds and words with infants or imitating their sounds but at other times remain silent in direct interactions with infants. Teachers occasionally attempt to involve infants by speaking directly to them or responding to them. Teachers initiate sounds to encourage infants to make sounds, but this happens only intermittently or with only a few infants. For example, when a teacher and infant are playing with a toy train, the teacher says "choo choo" in an attempt to get the infant to imitate the sound. When another infant begins to make the same sound, the teacher does not respond. Teachers sometimes imitate an infant's babble, but there are times when infants' sounds are not repeated. For instance, a teacher imitates an infant saying "dada," but at other times infants' sounds are not repeated.

Teachers sometimes provide words or extend infants' communication attempts but other times do not add language to those attempts. On occasion, teachers engage in back-and-forth verbal exchanges with infants, but this is not typical. At times, teachers acknowledge infants' sounds as a communication attempt or add words to their sounds, but at other times those attempts are missed or ignored. Teachers occasionally use specific and/or descriptive words in response to infants' communicative attempts, such as "It looks like you want the pacifier" or "Are you saying hi to your friend?" Teachers sometimes involve infants in back-and-forth verbal exchanges, but at other times this does not happen. For example, a teacher asks a question directly to an infant but then answers his or her own question or does not pause or make eye contact to encourage babbling or sounds in turn taking.

High Early Language Support (6, 7)

Teachers consistently describe their own and infants' actions during activities and routines. Teachers regularly comment on events happening in the classroom. Teachers' classroom language often includes descriptive and variable words, spoken in complete sentences. During free play and routines such as diapering and snack, teachers frequently use language in varying ways. Teachers regularly use words to describe what they are doing, linking words to actions. For example, a teacher says, "I'm putting music on" as the CD starts. Teachers also regularly provide words for infants' actions such as, "Brandon, you're waving your arms to music, like the branches of a tree." Teachers often speak using a variety of nouns, verbs, adverbs, adjectives, prepositions, and other forms of language in complete sentences in their conversations and interactions with infants. Teachers consistently label objects (e.g., two trucks, dump trucks) as well as numbers and colors, using descriptive and specific words.

Teachers frequently encourage infants to verbalize by initiating sounds and words with infants or imitating sounds expressed by infants. Teachers regularly attempt to support infants' language by encouraging them to talk or responding to their vocalizations by imitating sounds or repeating words. For example, a teacher says "ooh!" after an infant squeals with excitement. Teachers consistently repeat sounds infants make. For example, a teacher repeats "la la la" after the infant says it.

Teachers often extend infants' communication attempts by adding words to actions and sounds. Teachers consistently engage in back-and-forth verbal exchanges with infants, using pauses and eye contact to encourage turn taking. Teachers consistently respond to infants' vocalizations and actions with words that build on the initial communication. For example, a teacher says, "Bless you! That was a big sneeze!" after an infant sneezes, or "Does your blanket make you sleepy?" when an infant yawns after being wrapped in a blanket. Teachers regularly add on to infants' sounds and engage in language turn-taking behaviors. For example, the teacher hears an infant say "da" or squeak while looking at a book. The teacher extends this by saying "dog" and pointing to the picture of the dog in the book. The teacher then pauses and waits for the infant to communicate again. When the infant makes the "da" sound again the teacher extends it and says, "Yes, dog! Dogs go woof woof!"

References

Bernier, A., Carlson, S.M., & Whipple, N. (2010). From external regulation: Early parenting precursors of young children's executive functioning. *Child Development, 81*(1), 326–339.

Bogard, K., & Takanishi, R. (2005). PK–3: An aligned and coordinated approach to education for children 3 to 8 years old. *Social Policy Report, 42*(3), 1–24.

Bowlby, R. (2007). Babies and toddlers in non-parental daycare can avoid stress and anxiety if they develop a lasting secondary attachment bond with one carer who is consistently accessible to them. *Attachment and Human Development, 9*(4), 307–319.

Burchinal, M., Vernon-Feagans, L., Cox, M., & Key Family Life Project Investigators. (2008). Cumulative social risk, parenting, and infant development in rural low-income communities. *Parenting: Science and Practice, 8,* 41–69.

Cassibba, R., Van IJzendoorn, M.H., & D'Odorico, L. (2000). Attachment and play in child care centres: Reliability and validity of the attachment Q-sort for mothers and professional caregivers in Italy. *International Journal of Behavioral Development, 24*(2), 241–255.

Copple, C., & Bredekamp, S. (Eds.). (2009). *Developmentally appropriate practice in early childhood programs serving children from birth through age 8* (3rd ed.). Washington, DC: National Association for the Education of Young Children.

Essa, E.L., Favre, K., & Thweatt, S. (1999). Continuity of care for infants and toddlers. *Early Child Development and Care, 148*(1), 11–19.

Feldman, R., Eidelman, A.I., & Rotenberg, N. (2004). Parenting stress, infant emotional regulation, maternal sensitivity, and the cognitive development of triplets: A model for parent and child influences in a unique ecology. *Child Development, 75*(6), 1774–1791.

Howes, C., & Hamilton, C.E. (1992). Children's relationships with child care teachers: Stability and concordance with parental attachments. *Child Development, 63*(4), 867–878.

Howes, C., Hamilton, C.E., & Philipsen, L.C. (1998). Stability and continuity of child–caregiver and child–peer relations. *Child Development, 69*(2), 418–426.

Howes, C., & Smith, E.W. (1995). Relations among child care quality, teacher behavior, children's play activities, emotional security, and cognitive activity in child care. *Early Childhood Research Quarterly, 10*(4), 381–404.

Hamre, B.K., & Pianta, R.C. (2007). Learning opportunities in preschool and early elementary classrooms. In R.C. Pianta, M.J. Cox, & K.L. Snow (Eds.), *School readiness and the transition to kindergarten in the era of accountability* (pp. 49–83). Baltimore, MD: Paul H. Brookes Publishing Co.

Ispa, J.M., Fine, M.A., Halgunseth, L.C., Harper, S., Robinson, J., Boyce, L.,…Brady Smith, C. (2004). Maternal intrusiveness, maternal warmth, and mother–toddler relationship outcomes: Variations across low-income ethnic and acculturation groups. *Child Development, 75*(6), 1613–1631.

Kochanska, G., Furman, D.R., Aksan, N., & Dunbar, S.B. (2005). Pathways to conscience: Early mother–child mutually responsive orientation and children's moral emotion, conduct and cognition. *Journal of Child Psychology and Psychiatry, 46*(1), 19–34.

La Paro, K.M., Hamre, B.K., & Pianta, R.C. (2012). *Classroom Assessment Scoring System® (CLASS™) manual, Toddler.* Baltimore, MD: Paul H. Brookes Publishing Co.

Lally, J.R. (2010). School readiness begins in infancy. *Kappan, 92*(3), 17–21.

Mashburn, A.J., Pianta, R., Hamre, B.K., Downer, J.T., Barbarin, O., Bryant, D.,...Howes, C. (2008). Measures of classroom quality in pre-kindergarten and children's development of academic, language, and social skills. *Child Development, 79, 732–749.*

Mitchell-Copeland, J., Denham, S.A., & DeMulder, E.K. (1997). Q-sort assessment of child–teacher attachment relationships and social competence in the preschool. *Early Education and Development, 8*(1), 27–39.

Morrison, F.J., & Connor, C.M. (2002). Understanding schooling effects on early literacy: A working research strategy. *Journal of School Psychology, 40*(6), 493–500.

National Institute of Child Health and Human Development Early Child Care Research Network (1996). Characteristics of infant child care: Factors contributing to positive caregiving. *Early Childhood Research Quarterly, 11,* 269–306.

National Institute of Child Health and Human Development Early Child Care Research Network (2000a). Characteristics and quality of child care for toddlers and preschoolers. *Journal of Applied Developmental Science, 4,* 116–135.

National Institute of Child Health and Human Development Early Child Care Research Network. (2000b). The relation of child care to cognitive and language development. *Child Development, 71,* 960–980.

National Institute of Child Health and Human Development Early Child Care Research Network. (2001, April). *Further explorations of the detected effects of quantity of early child care on socioemotional adjustment.* Paper presented at the biennial meeting of the Society for Research in Child Development, Minneapolis, MN.

National Institute of Child Health and Human Development Early Child Care Research Network. (2003). Does amount of time spent in child care predict socioemotional adjustment during the transition to kindergarten? *Child Development, 74,* 976–1005.

Nelson, C.A., & Bosquet, M. (2005). Neurobiology of fetal and infant development: Implications for infant mental health. In C.H. Zeanah (Ed.), *Handbook of infant mental health* (2nd ed., pp. 37–59). New York, NY: Guilford Press.

Pianta, R.C., La Paro, K.M., & Hamre, B.K. (2008). *Classroom Assessment Scoring System® (CLASS™) manual, Pre-K.* Baltimore, MD: Paul H. Brookes Publishing Co.

Raikes, H., & Edwards, C.P. (2009). Staying in step: Supporting relationships with families of infants and toddlers. *Young Children, 64*(5), 50–55.

Rutter, M., & Maughan, B. (2002). School effectiveness findings, 1979–2002. *Journal of School Psychology, 40*(6), 451–475.

Schertz, H.H., & Odom, S.L. (2007). Promoting joint attention in toddlers with autism: A parent-mediated developmental model. *Journal of Autism and Developmental Disorders, 37,* 1562–1575.

Schore, A.N. (2005). Attachment, affect regulation, and the developing right brain: Linking developmental neuroscience to pediatrics. *Pediatrics in Review, 26*(6), 204–217.

Sroufe, L.A. (1996). *Emotional development: The organization of emotional life in the early years.* New York, NY: Cambridge University Press.

Thompson, R.A. (2006). Nurturing developing brains, minds, and hearts. In R. Lally & P. Mangione (Eds.), *Concepts of care: 20 essays on infant/toddler development and learning* (pp. 47–52). Sausalito, CA: WestEd.

Thompson, R.A. (2009). "Doing what doesn't come naturally." *Zero to Three, 30*(2), 33–39.

van IJzendoorn, M.H., Sagi, A., & Lambermon, M.W. (1992). The multiple caretaker paradox: Data from Holland and Israel. *New Directions for Child and Adolescent Development, 1992*(57), 5–24.

Vandell, D.L., Belsky, J., Burchinal, M., Steinberg, L., Vandergrift, N., & National Institute of Child Health and Human Development Early Child Care Research Network. (2010). Do effects of early child care extend to age 15 years? Results from the NICHD Study of Early Child Care and Youth Development. *Child Development, 81*(3), 737–756.

Vygotsky, L.S. (1998). *The collected works of L.S. Vygotsky: Child psychology* (Vol. 5). (R.W. Rieber, Ed.). New York, NY: Plenum.

ZERO TO THREE. (2008). *Caring for infants and toddlers in groups: Developmentally appropriate practice* (2nd ed.). Washington, DC: Author.

CLASS Infant
Technical Appendix

This technical appendix presents the psychometric properties of the Infant version of the Classroom Assessment Scoring System® (CLASS®), including descriptive statistics and initial validity findings. The CLASS Infant is an observational assessment of interactions between caregivers and infants in settings providing care for young children between 6 weeks and 18 months of age. For the purposes of this tool and consistency with other versions of the CLASS, the focus of observations are described as "teacher–child interactions," including the range of nonparental adults providing care for infants. For similar purposes, caregiving settings are described as "classrooms" and include a variety of settings ranging from center-based settings to family child care settings. The psychometric properties of CLASS Infant described herein are based on observations in predominantly center-based infant classrooms; however, samples of observations include less formal care settings, and evidence supports the use of the tool across the range of settings in which infants receive care. Challenges and constraints to using CLASS Infant across formal and informal care settings are addressed in the previous chapters as well as in CLASS Infant training, and those guidelines should be referenced when considering use in any setting.

CLASS INFANT DEVELOPMENT

The CLASS Infant is an age-related downward extension of the CLASS Pre-K and Toddler observational assessments of teacher–child interactions in classroom settings (La Paro, Hamre, & Pianta, 2012; Pianta, La Paro, & Hamre, 2008). The development of the CLASS Infant was informed by the extensive research and implementation experience associated with the CLASS Pre-K and Toddler, as well as prior research on developmentally appropriate teacher–child interactions in child care settings serving infants and toddlers (Copple & Bredekamp, 2009; Hamre & Pianta, 2007; National Institute of Child Health and Human Development Early Child Care Research Network, 1996). As noted previously, to remain consistent with previous versions of the CLASS, we use the term *teacher* to refer to any caregiver in a setting providing child care to children between the ages of 6 weeks and 18 months. *Classrooms* refer to settings ranging from more formal center-based care to informal care provided in homes and family child care settings in which the adult observed may actually be a parent of one or more of the children present.

An underlying assumption of the theoretical and measurement framework informing the several versions of the CLASS (i.e., Infant, Toddler, Pre-K, K–3) is heterotypic continuity in effective teacher–child interactions across varying age levels. In this use, *heterotypic continuity* refers to the underlying similarity and significance for children's development of features of teacher–child interaction across varying ages, even when the specific examples or behaviors indicating those features may be different for different-age children. More specifically, this means that the dimensions used in the CLASS to define and assess effective teacher–child interactions are similar across the infant, toddler, and preschool periods. The behaviors of teachers that indicate these dimensions, however, are specific to particular developmental levels or age groups (i.e., infant versus toddler, toddler versus preschool). In other words, although Teacher Sensitivity is a critical dimension of effective teacher–child interaction having value for preschoolers or for infants, the specific behaviors through which Teacher Sensitivity may be demonstrated in practice may differ across ages. As another example, the types of language exchanges between teachers and infants or toddlers or preschoolers may vary with regard to their value for promoting language development, and thus, the behaviors teachers engage in to support developing language may be different across these ages. In most cases of aligning CLASS dimensions across ages or developmental periods, the name of the dimension remains the same (e.g., Teacher Sensitivity); however, for the CLASS Infant, the data and theoretical support suggested some nomenclature shifts in names of dimensions. For example, CLASS Infant describes interactions that promote language development in terms of the dimension of Early Language Support, whereas the Toddler and Pre-K manuals describe this feature of interaction using the dimension of Language Modeling.

Development of the manual was an iterative process that first began in the review of the CLASS Toddler and CLASS Pre-K and of pertinent research literature on key aspects of adult–infant interactions that could be observed reliably and for which there was evidence of prediction of infant and toddler developmental outcomes (Copple & Bredekamp, 2009; Hamre & Pianta, 2007; National Institute of Child Health and Human Development Early Child Care Research Network, 1996). With a refined set of relevant features of teacher–infant interaction, the team of authors reviewed videotaped samples of teacher–infant interactions in classroom settings serving infants. This process resulted in the first, early pilot-stage version of the manual. A panel of experts on infant development then reviewed this early pilot version of the manual and provided feedback on 1) the extent to which the set of dimensions presented in the manual was sufficiently relevant and comprehensive, and 2) the clarity and specificity with which behaviors were described, so as to facilitate accurate and reliable observations. A round of revisions to the manual followed.

Subsequent to those revisions, a second panel of experts with expertise in child care viewed selected videos and used this version of the manual to assign codes to the interactions present in the videos. This process resulted in improved definitions and descriptions for the CLASS Infant dimensions as well as further refinement of behavioral anchors for dimension scale points. Following these refinements, the manual was piloted to further improve clarity of the tool, gather information helpful to users' decision making and implementation, and collect initial reliability and validity data (discussed in more detail later in this appendix).

Following this pilot stage, a final round of CLASS Infant revisions was completed. All pilot studies intentionally conducted observations during both routine care and playtime and indicated that the manual and behavioral descriptions were applicable in the different activity settings. This final version of the CLASS Infant includes four dimensions of effective teacher–infant interaction in classrooms providing care to infants.

DATA SOURCES FOR THE TECHNICAL APPENDIX

To present the psychometric properties of the CLASS Infant, this technical appendix draws on data from several studies in which the CLASS Infant was applied in settings serving children ages 6 weeks to 18 months, each briefly described in the following subsections. As noted in the descriptions, the studies providing data are diverse and illustrative in nature but do not reflect a representative sample of infant child care settings. Despite this limitation, when considered in the aggregate, the samples provide a rich opportunity to examine psychometric properties of the CLASS Infant. All participating study data collectors received training from experienced trainers and met standards for reliability. Across studies, multiple adults were typically observed within a classroom. For all data reported, observations were conducted and reported at the classroom level (i.e., ratings were not assigned for dyadic teacher–infant interactions but as characteristic of teacher–infant interactions across all infants in the setting).

Child Development Resources

Primary investigators: Virginia Infant & Toddler Specialist Network

Number of classrooms: 56 (49 center-based child care; 7 family-based child care)

Location: Various communities in Virginia

Time span: June 2012 to March 2013

Observation procedure: Trained research staff observed each classroom in the morning.

Educare

Primary investigators: Lisa St. Clair, Ed.D., Barb Jackson, Ph.D., Amanda Stein, Todd Jackson, Heather Horsely, Marsha Hawley, Nancy File, Marcela Sweeny, Pam Costakis, and Karen Freel

Number of classrooms: 28

Location: Six Educare sites in the Midwest

Time span: September 2012 to May 2013

Observation procedure: Trained research staff observed each classroom in the morning.

United Way, Miami

Primary investigator: Christine R. Hughes, Ph.D.

Number of classrooms: 53

Location: Miami, Florida

Time span: December 2012 to January 2013

Observation procedure: Trained research staff observed each classroom in the morning for a minimum of six cycles in each room. All assessors were Spanish and English bilinguals and took into account all interactions in both languages.

University of Massachusetts, Boston

Primary investigators: Angi Stone MacDonald, Lisa Van Thiel, Jennifer Kearns Fox, and Lynne Mendee, University of Massachusetts, Boston

Number of classrooms: 27 (6 play groups; 5 family child care; 16 center based)

Location: Six sites in eastern Massachusetts

Time span: Spring 2013

Observation procedure: Trained research staff conducted observations in settings in which the majority of children in the group were infants.

University of North Carolina, Greensboro

Primary investigators: National Center Rated License Assessment Project, University of North Carolina, Greensboro

Number of classrooms: 97

Location: Urban and suburban areas of North Carolina

Time span: Summer 2012 to Fall 2012

Observation procedure: Trained research staff observed each classroom in the morning for a minimum of four cycles in each room. Cycles were completed continuously and included all usual play and learning activities, routines, and transitions.

University of Virginia

Primary investigator: Jennifer LoCasale-Crouch, Ph.D., University of Virginia

Number of classrooms: 30 (all center-based child care)

Location: Virginia

Time span: Fall 2010

Observation procedure: Trained research staff observed each classroom once for approximately 3–4 hours. Most observations began at approximately 8:30 a.m., when the majority of infants were present.

DESCRIPTIVE INFORMATION

The following subsections provide detailed information about the CLASS Infant psychometric properties. Descriptive data are presented initially at the individual study level, and then data sets are combined for analyses that follow to utilize a larger sample size for increased stability in results.

Means and Variation on the CLASS Infant Dimensions

Table A.1 provides means, standard deviations, and ranges for CLASS scores from the six aforementioned studies. Note that these data are not nationally representative and are intended only to provide examples of scores across several studies rather than national averages.

Looking at the descriptive data from these six studies, several findings are noteworthy. First, in ranges for assigned ratings for each sample, there is adequate distribution of ratings across the 7-point scale(s) for each dimension. In addition, Relational Climate and Teacher Sensitivity tend to be rated slightly higher than Facilitated Exploration and Early Language Support.

Associations Among the CLASS Infant Dimensions

Table A.2 reports correlations between CLASS dimensions. These correlations are derived from all available data, aggregating across all of the six aforementioned studies in order to increase sample size on which the correlations were based. All of the CLASS dimensions are moderately to highly correlated in the six-study aggregate sample. In the context of the overall pattern of moderate-to-high correlations, Relational Climate is most closely related to Teacher Sensitivity, whereas Facilitated Exploration is most strongly related to Early Language Support.

Prior analyses on one of the CLASS pilot samples obtained during development of the assessment (Jamison et al., in press) suggested that the CLASS Infant dimensions may represent a single factor. Internal consistency estimates for a composite single score obtained from averaging the four CLASS dimensions were calculated separately for each of the six study samples and for the entire six-study aggregate. Cronbach's alpha for this

Table A.1. Descriptive statistics (*M, SD,* range) on Classroom Assessment Scoring System® (CLASS®) Infant across six samples

		CDR	Educare	Miami	UMB	UNC	UVA
	N	56	28	53	27	97	30
Relational Climate	*M*	4.11	5.32	5.75	5.99	5.04	5.07
	SD	(1.23)	(1.45)	(0.88)	(0.81)	(1.02)	(0.98)
	Range	1.00–6.00	1.75–7.00	2.00–7.00	4.50–7.00	2.00–6.67	2.50–6.33
Teacher Sensitivity	*M*	4.09	5.22	5.71	5.71	4.75	5.13
	SD	(1.28)	(1.50)	(0.98)	(0.80)	(1.16)	(0.93)
	Range	1.00–6.00	1.25–7.00	2.00–7.00	4.00–7.00	1.50–7.00	2.75–7.00
Facilitated Exploration	*M*	3.38	4.27	4.30	3.53	3.68	4.02
	SD	(1.18)	(1.71)	(1.33)	(1.46)	(1.07)	(1.08)
	Range	1.00–6.00	1.00–6.50	2.00–7.00	1.00–6.50	1.00–6.50	2.00–6.50
Early Language Support	*M*	3.23	3.97	3.52	3.52	3.31	3.89
	SD	(1.08)	(1.75)	(1.26)	(1.10)	(1.19)	(1.02)
	Range	1.00–6.00	1.00–6.75	1.00–6.00	1.89–6.25	1.00–6.25	2.25–6.50

Key: CDR, Child Development Resources; Miami, United Way, Miami; UMB, University of Massachusetts, Boston; UNC, University of North Carolina, Greensboro; UVA, University of Virginia.

four-dimension composite ranged from 0.73 to 0.97 (the highest drawn from the aggregate sample), indicating moderate to strong internal consistency. After combining the six data-sets available, a confirmatory factor analysis (CFA) was conducted to measure the extent to which a single, overall dimension reflected the pattern of covariance among the four separate dimensions. Results for the CFA are reported in Table A.3 and indicate that the one-factor solution fits the current data best, and the model fit is greatly improved when the dimensions Relational Climate and Teacher Sensitivity are correlated, indicating the relatively greater association between these two dimensions than between them and Facilitated Exploration or Early Language Support. Results from this CFA, and the high levels of internal consistency reliability obtained in analyses just described for an overall composite based on the four dimensions' average, suggest that a single overall score reflects quite well the CLASS Infant assessment of the quality of teacher–infant interactions in settings serving infants. This overall score is described as Responsive Caregiving and is computed as an average of the four dimensions' ratings once they are averaged across cycles.

Table A.2. Correlations among Classroom Assessment Scoring System® (CLASS®) Infant dimensions from six studies (*N* = 291)

	1	2	3	4
1. Relational Climate	—			
2. Teacher Sensitivity	.87	—		
3. Facilitated Exploration	.63	.69	—	
4. Early Language Support	.61	.66	.81	—

Table A.3. Confirmatory factor analysis (CFA) for Classroom Assessment Scoring System®
(CLASS®) Infant data pooling across six studies (N = 291)

Factor loadings	(CFA without cross loading)	(CFA cross loading RC and TS)
Relational Climate	.90	.69
Teacher Sensitivity	.95	.75
Facilitated Exploration	.75	.92
Early Language Support	.73	.88
Fit indices		
Chi-square (df)	141.78 (2)	.78 (1)
RMSEA	.49	.00
RMSEA C.I.	.424–.560	0–.148
CFI	.85	1.0
SRMR	.075	.003

Key: RC, Relational Climate; TS, Teacher Sensitivity.

To What Extent Are the CLASS Ratings Stable Across Cycles?

Current recommendations include conducting as many CLASS observation cycles as possible to increase the likelihood that the observation is reliable. In four studies where data were available at the cycle level, correlations across four cycles were conducted and are presented in Table A.4. Each column represents the correlation between a cycle and the average of four cycles. As expected, correlations increase as more cycles are added, but they also reflect the highly stable nature of teacher–infant interactions in settings serving infants, such that very little stability is added to scores after two cycles are completed.

VALIDITY

Face Validity of the CLASS Infant

The CLASS Infant was developed based on an extensive literature review and observed practices in early childhood care and education. The dimensions were derived based on constructs identified in classroom observation, literature on effective teaching practices, and extensive piloting. Throughout this process, various experts in early childhood educa-

Table A.4. Correlations between cycle and total score for Classroom Assessment Scoring System®
(CLASS®) Infant dimensions in four studies (N = 182)

CLASS dimensions	Cycle 1 with Cycles 1–4	Cycle 1 and 2 with Cycles 1–4	Cycles 1, 2, and 3 with Cycles 1–4
Relational Climate	.92	.96	.99
Teacher Sensitivity	.90	.96	.98
Facilitated Exploration	.89	.95	.98
Early Language Support	.91	.96	.98

Note: All correlations are significant at p < .001.

Table A.5. Correlations between the Classroom Assessment Scoring System® (CLASS®) Infant dimensions and Infant/Toddler Environment Rating Scale–Revised Edition (ITERS-R; Harms, Cryer, & Clifford, 2006) Structural and Process Scales in three studies (N = 147)

	ITERS-R Structural Scales		ITERS-R Process Scales		
	Space and furnishings	Program structure	Listening and talking	Interaction	Overall ITERS-R score
Relational Climate		.46	.56	.57	.58
Teacher Sensitivity	.49	.48	.59	.58	.60
Facilitated Exploration	.37	.41	.52	.48	.50
Early Language Support	.34	.28	.46	.35	.42

Note: All correlations are significant at $p < .001$.

tion agreed that the CLASS Infant measures aspects of the early childhood classroom that are important for promoting child development, suggesting considerable face validity. Experts also attended to the comprehensiveness of the CLASS Infant dimensions, reporting good coverage of interaction features believed to be relevant for promoting infant development.

Associations of the CLASS Infant with Infant/Toddler Environment Rating Scale–Revised Edition: Criterion Validity

Criterion validity involves the extent to which a measure is associated with other measures of similar constructs. Table A.5 presents results from analyses examining associations between the CLASS dimensions and specific structural and process scales as well as the overall score derived from the Infant/Toddler Environment Rating Scale–Revised Edition (ITERS-R; Harms, Cryer, & Clifford, 2006), the most commonly used observational measure of quality in infant classrooms. Results suggest that CLASS Infant dimensions are moderately correlated with the process/interaction scales and, not surprisingly, demonstrate lower associations with the ITERS-R structural scales. This expected pattern provides initial evidence of both convergent and discriminant validity for CLASS Infant.

SUMMARY

Based on the current data gathered across studies, including observations of 291 different settings providing care for infants between 6 weeks and 18 months, findings indicate that CLASS Infant scores reflect the range of possible scale points, with patterns of means and variability similar to other versions of the CLASS. In addition, in examining correlations among CLASS Infant dimensions and analyses to explore the properties of a four-dimension composite score, evidence supports the use of a single domain, Responsive Caregiving, to characterize overall quality of teacher–infant interaction based on the four CLASS Infant dimensions. Finally, the data presented here indicate that CLASS Infant dimension scores demonstrate expected convergent and divergent validity in correlations with the ITERS-R, such that relations in the CLASS Infant are strongest between scales assessing setting processes and lower when involving CLASS Infant and scales from the ITERS-R that reflect structural features of settings. Thus, overall, the CLASS Infant provides developmentally relevant, reliable, and valid information about teacher–infant interactions within the range of formal and informal early childhood classroom settings serving infants. Consequently, the CLASS Infant may be a useful tool for researchers, program administrators, teachers, and policy makers seeking a standardized measure of effective teacher–infant interaction for use in this developmental period. This Technical Manual Appendix will be updated regularly at www.teachstone.org and www.brookespublishing.com/class-infant.

REFERENCES

Copple, C., & Bredekamp, S. (Eds.). (2009). *Developmentally appropriate practice in early childhood programs serving children from birth through age 8* (3rd ed.). Washington, DC: National Association for the Education of Young Children.

Hamre, B.K., & Pianta, R.C. (2007). Learning opportunities in preschool and early elementary classrooms. In R. Pianta, M. Cox, & K. Snow (Eds.), *School readiness and the transition to kindergarten in the era of accountability* (pp. 49–84). Baltimore, MD: Paul H. Brookes Publishing Co.

Harms, T., Cryer, D., & Clifford, R.M. (2006). *Infant/Toddler Environment Rating Scale–Revised Edition*. New York, NY: Teachers College Press.

Jamison, K.R., Cabell, S.Q., LoCasale-Crouch, J., Hamre, B.K., & Pianta, R.C. (in press). CLASS, Infant: An observational measure to assess teacher–infant interactions in center-based child care. *Early Education and Development.*

La Paro, K.M., Hamre, B.K., & Pianta, R.C. (2012). *Classroom Assessment Scoring System® (CLASS™) manual, Toddler.* Baltimore, MD: Paul H. Brookes Publishing Co.

National Institute of Child Health and Human Development Early Child Care Research Network. (1996). Characteristics of infant child care: Factors contributing to positive caregiving. *Early Childhood Research Quarterly, 11,* 269–306.

Pianta, R.C., La Paro, K.M., & Hamre, B.K. (2008). *Classroom Assessment Scoring System® (CLASS™) manual, Pre-K.* Baltimore, MD: Paul H. Brookes Publishing Co.

Index

Pages followed by *t* indicate tables; those followed by *f* indicate figures.

Your quick-guide to  CLASS. products

hools across the country trust the CLASS® observational tool—the most accurate, efficient way to assess the quality
interactions between children and teachers. With versions for Infant, Toddler, Pre-K, and K–3 classrooms, the
LASS® tool

- **Is both valid and reliable**, proven through research and testing in diverse early childhood settings
- **Highlights areas of strength and areas for growth**—ideal for guiding improvement efforts
- **Addresses your program's most urgent needs**, including accountability efforts, professional development, program planning, and research

EW! CLASS® Infant

eveloped for use with children from birth to 18 months, the NEW CLASS® Infant tool assesses 4 dimensions of teacher–
ild interaction: relational climate, teacher sensitivity, facilitated exploration, and early language support.

Manual—US$54.95
Stock #: BA-76047
2014
ISBN 978-1-59757-604-7

Forms—US$30.00
Stock #: BA-76054
2014
ISBN 978-1-59857-605-4
Package of 10

LASS® Toddler

r use with children from 15–36 months, the toddler version covers two domains of teacher-child interaction: Emotional
d Behavior Support (5 dimensions) and Engaged Support for Learning (3 dimensions).

Toddler Manual—US$54.95
Stock #: BA-72599
2012
ISBN 978-1-59857-259-9

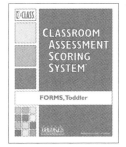

Toddler Forms—US$30.00
Stock #: BA-72605
2012
ISBN 978-1-59857-260-5
Package of 10

CLASS® Observation Training is an essential prerequisite for accurate use of the CLASS® tool.
Learn more about it at www.teachstone.com/training-programs.

CLASS® Pre-K, CLASS® K–3

Both CLASS® Pre-K and CLASS® K–3 focus on three key domains of teacher–student interaction—Emotional Support, Classroom Organization, and Instructional Support that matter for young children's growth and development. And now Spanish-speaking CLASS® observers can use the Spanish CLASS® Manual and Forms, Pre-K as they observe early childhood classrooms.

Manuals

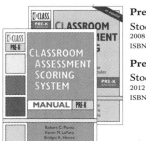

Pre-K English—US$54.95
Stock #: BA-69414
2008
ISBN 978-1-55766-941-4

Pre-K Spanish—US$54.95
Stock #: BA-72384
2012
ISBN 978-1-59857-238-4

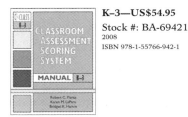

K–3—US$54.95
Stock #: BA-69421
2008
ISBN 978-1-55766-942-1

Forms

Pre-K–3 English—US$30
Stock #: BA-69438
2008
ISBN 978-1-55766-943-8
Package of 10

Pre-K Spanish—US$30.0
Stock #: BA-72360
2012
ISBN 978-1-59857-236-0
Package of 10

CLASS® Dimensions Overview

Available in convenient packages of 5, this tri-fold laminated sheet shows evaluators an at-a-glance overview of the CLASS® dimensions.

Each Dimensions Overview—US$30.00 • 6 pages, tri-fold • package of 5

Infant
Stock #: BA-76061
2014
ISBN 978-1-59857-606-1

Toddler
Stock #: BA-72612
2012
ISBN 978-1-59857-261-2

Pre-K–3 English
Stock #: BA-70885
2009
ISBN 978-1-59857-088-5

Pre-K Spanish
Stock #: BA-72353
2012
ISBN 978-1-59857-235-3

CLASS® Dimensions Guide

Introduce teachers to the dimensions of the CLASS® tool with these concise guides, each with practical teaching tips. A great way to get teachers on board with the CLASS® observation!

Each guide—US$19.95 • 2011 • 28 pages • 8 ½ x 11 • saddle-stitched

Infant English
Stock #: BA-78119
ISBN 978-1-59857-811-9

Infant Spanish
Stock #: BA-79666
ISBN 978-1-59857-966-6

K-3(English only)
Stock #: BA-72308
ISBN 978-1-59857-230-8

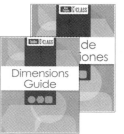

Toddler English
Stock #: BA-72292
ISBN 978-1-59857-229-2

Toddler Spanish
Stock #: BA-76078
ISBN 978-1-59857-607-8

Pre-K English
Stock #: BA-72278
ISBN 978-1-59857-227-8

Pre-K Spanish
Stock #: BA-72285
ISBN 978-1-59857-228-5